An Arabian Portfolio

An Arabian Portfolio

Photographs by ROBERT AZZI
Introduction by H.E. SHAIKH AHMED ZAKI YAMANI
Minister of Petroleum and Mineral Resources, Saudi Arabia

 Addison House   Danbury, New Hampshire

Photographs © 1976 by Robert Azzi

Photographs on pages 55, 59,
63, 71, 72 by Robert Azzi
© National Geographic Magazine,
Washington D.C., USA

ISBN 2 85119 010 5

Library of Congress n° 77 - 74753

Printed by Draeger, Montrouge France

Published in the U.S.A.
by Addison House, Danbury, N.H.

Table of Contents

Dedicated
to the memory of my father
Alexander
and to the memory of
Charles Philbrick

To my family

To the Mountain Lady

To His Excellency Shaikh
Ahmed Zaki Yamani

To Makram Alamuddin and Omar Hamza

To those friends named Abdul
Rahman, Abu Faisal, Al Alami, Al Faisal,
Alghanim, Ali Reza, Anderson,
Barbey, Bator, Battal, Bauval,
Brandreth, Chalmers, Close, Cobey,
Crawford, Dickson, Drushall, Dubois,
Egee, Froriep, Gilka, Grandy, Hardtke,
Hargate, Haymann, Hebert, Hoagland,
Hoye, Hughes, Jackson, Jashanmal,
Jenkins, Jones, Joyce, Kaynor,
Kellings, Khaberi, Khalife, Leach,
Mamarbachi, Markham, Matthew, Mugar,
Nusseibeh, Obeid, Ockrent, O'Grady,
Pam, Peyton,
Philbrick, Roberts, Roosevelt, Rossi,
Rowland, Sams, Smith, Stewart,
Talmage, Tracy, Yateem, and Young

To Rene Bürri for his invaluable
assistance with the design of the book

To my associates and the staff of
Magnum Photos

To Najwa-Grace Ibrahim

Thank you.

Preface

I cannot escape what I am.

As an American of Arab origin I have lived
in the Middle East since 1968,
discovering and embracing a people,
a religion and a culture
that belonged to my forebears—
and which now belongs to me.

This book
documents some of those discoveries.
It is a collection of photographs, perhaps
uncommon, always personal—a portfolio—
that expresses what I feel about
the Arabian Peninsula.

It is not a comprehensive view.
I have chosen
to limit the photographs to those I feel most
closely represent my reactions
—visceral, visual perceptions—
to a people, a landscape, a land in flux.

Arabia.
The way it was.
The way it is.

The way I am.

R A

Introduction

Since time immemorial, the Arabian Peninsula has been a rich source of knowledge on which historians, archaelogists and anthropologists thrived. The many historical attractions that are to be found in Arabia today indicate the heights of civilization that were attained by the people of the Peninsula many thousands of years ago, and compete in their magnificence with the Pyramids of Egypt.

In the field of commerce, the people of the Peninsula had established international trading relationships with other nations in the world. The trade caravans of the Kingdom of Sheba in the South crossed the desert towards a number of countries in the North. Some of the traders went to settle in North Africa, where they built cities, which they named after their own home cities in Southern Arabia.

At a later stage, the tribe of Quraysh in Mecca engaged in extensive trade activities creating commercial links between India and Europe. Their caravans travelled eastwards in winter, where they bought the merchandise of the Indians, and northwards in summer, to points where they could meet the European merchants. The commercial activity of the Quraysh continued until the days of the Prophet Muhammad, who in his youth, engaged in this kind of international trade.

In the field of mining also, the ancient mines from which various minerals were extracted seem to confirm that the Arabian Peninsula was an exporter of minerals long before Christ, and that the mining activities had reached a high level of development.

However, the importance of the Arabian Peninsula to the world at large does not emanate from its ancient trading or mining activities — it emanates from two far more important contributions it made to the welfare of humanity — the Religion of Islam, and Oil.

To the Muslims of the world, who today exceed 600 million, Islam brought a complete way of life. It was Islam that enlightened the Arabs of the peninsula to the extent that enabled them to present to the world a civilization of a high order at a time when Europe and the rest of the world were still in the grip of dark ignorance. The Arabic origins of the names of such vital sciences as chemistry and algebra are reminders of the contribution of the Arabs to the sciences, while the invention of the nought and the Arabic numerals was the means by which they revolutionized arithmetic.

In spite of the difficult times that the Arabian Peninsula later went through, and the subjection of parts of it to long periods of colonialism, one characteristic of the inhabitants of the Arabian desert never fails to attract attention. That characteristic is a mental maturity that the Arabs of the desert, even the illiterate ones, possess. This quality is a great asset and an invaluable aid to them in facing the complexities of life with confidence. It is often reflected in the poetry in which they excel in composing impromptu and which combines the beauty of the Arabic language with the expressive powers of the Arab individual. When modern education came within their reach, they proved extraordinary abilities that never failed to attract admiration.

With the start of the age of enlightenment for the Arabs of the peninsula, their land started making its second historical contribution to the welfare of the world. This happened when oil started flowing in large quantities and it was proved that nearly half the entire oil reserves of the world lay beneath their sands. The extent to which the welfare of the world was going to depend on the Arabian Peninsula was recognized as considerable from the start, but with today's insatiable demand of the modern industrial countries for energy, that dependence has been greatly increased.

The economic progress of North America, Europe and Japan can only be maintained with the availability of the oil of the Peninsula. Oil from other sources, such as Alaska, the North Sea and the rest of the OPEC areas can only meet a part of the world's rising demand for energy, making the Arabian Peninsula the biggest single source on which the world can depend until modern technology achieves a breakthrough in the next century and provides an alternative source of energy. When that happens, the world will depend on Arabian oil as a raw material for its petrochemical industries.

God's bounty to the Arabs of the peninsula has been used with beneficial effects for the whole world. Guided by the principles of their Islamic faith, the people of the peninsula repeatedly demonstrated the sense of responsibility they feel towards others in the way they handled their increasing economic power. They chose to produce much more oil than warranted by their needs in order to meet the world's needs; they were almost the only deterrent within OPEC against oil prices rising to levels that would be ruinous to the world economy; and they gave record breaking grants-in-aid to the countries of the Third World.

The people of the peninsula, united by the Islamic faith and fortified, in as far as that may be possible, by their oil wealth, nevertheless face many big challenges. The future is by no means free of considerable difficulties. How are they going to use their spiritual and material resources in facing the future? They naturally aspire to the day when their human resources constitute a major part of their wealth, when they have enough scientists and researchers and engineers to shift their dependence from their oil to more permanent industrial foundations.

The road to these objectives is no doubt beset with many difficulties, but that is not the real challenge. The real challenge is whether the people of the peninsula will be able to achieve their long term objectives without loosing, in the process, their beautiful traditions, their great culture and above all, the spirit of their Islamic faith. Whether this challenge will be met with success or not, only the future will tell, although the anthropologists and the students of Islam and the Arabian Peninsula are almost unanimous in the belief that the spiritual legacy of the Arabs will not be sacrificed on the altar of material reconstruction.

The foregoing words are aimed to give a very brief sketch of the subject matter that Robert Azzi has succeeded so admirably in capturing in the pictures that constitute his «Arabian Portfolio». No matter how expressive words may be, they cannot tell the mind what pictures can. Mr. Azzi has used his vision and his cameras to portray the faces and feelings of a land undergoing tremendous development and change, while tenaciously holding fast to its cherished spiritual and cultural values. In many instances the ancient is seen side by side with the modern, while the emptiness of the Arabian desert is recorded to provide sharp contrast to the crowded and prosperous coastal cities.

This vivid work provides, in a way no written work can, what anyone who is interested in an area or a people but does not have the opportunity to see for oneself, seeks most: a picture as close to reality as possible. The result of Mr. Azzi's work says a great deal about the Arabian Peninsula, its history, its culture and its people. It constitutes a substantial and most welcome addition to the current efforts of a handful of sincere people who genuinely seek to bring the people of the Arabian Peninsula and the other nations of the world closer together.

لا إله إلا الله

The Rulers

الحكّام

Tradition

التقاليد

Resources

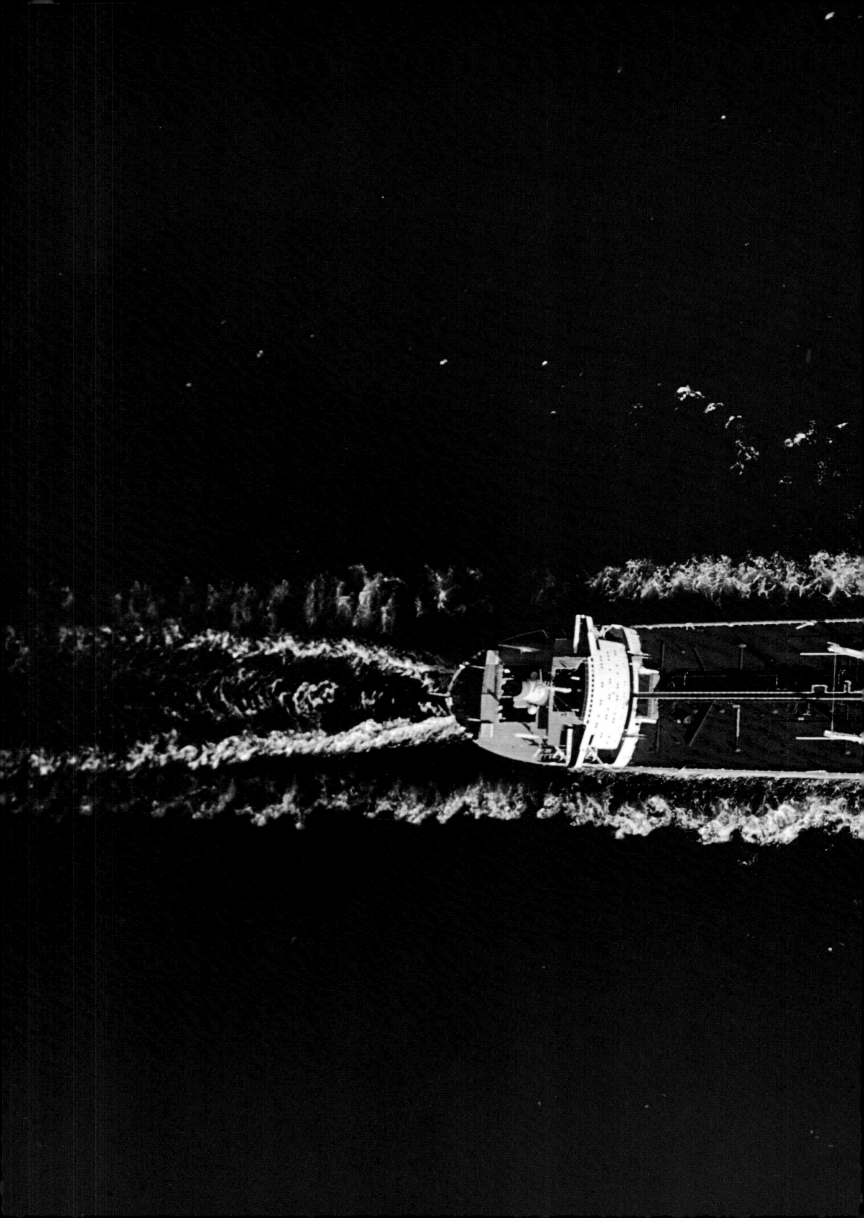

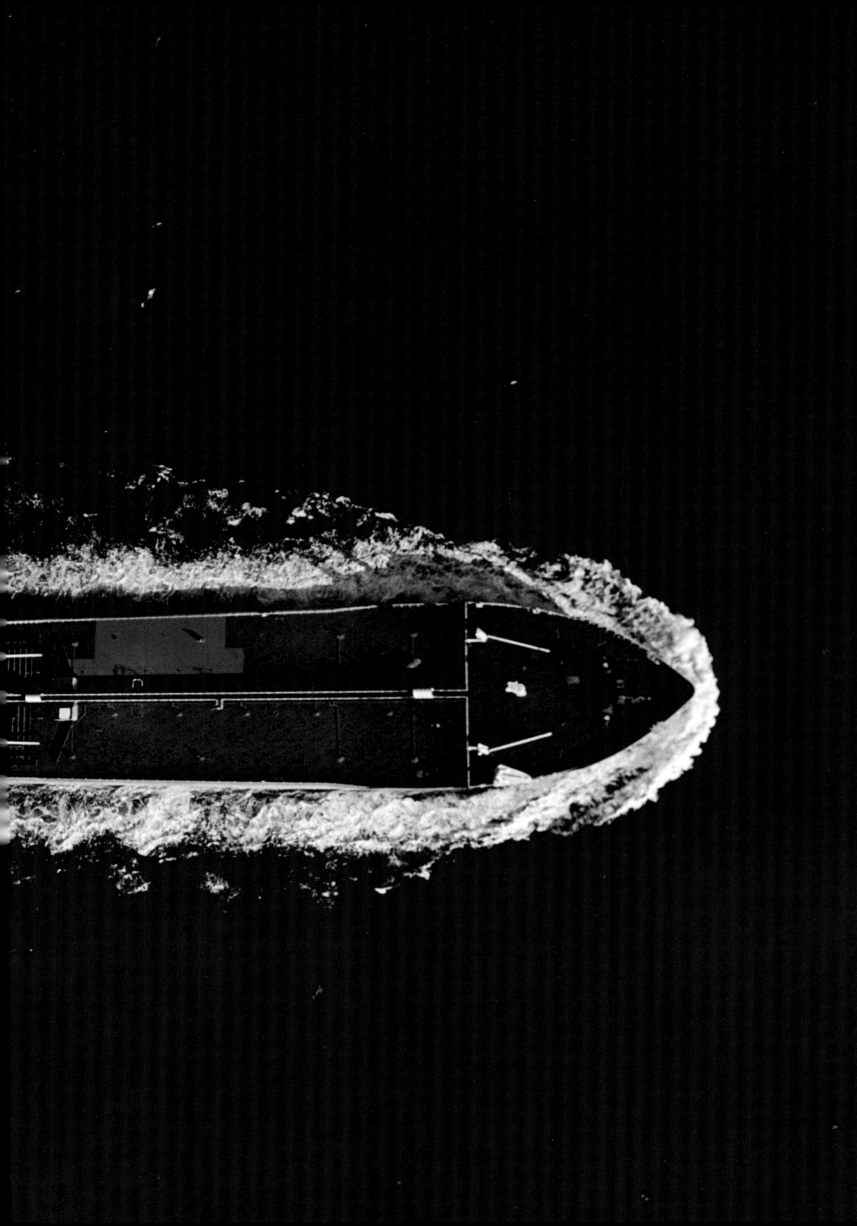

A New World

العالم الجديد

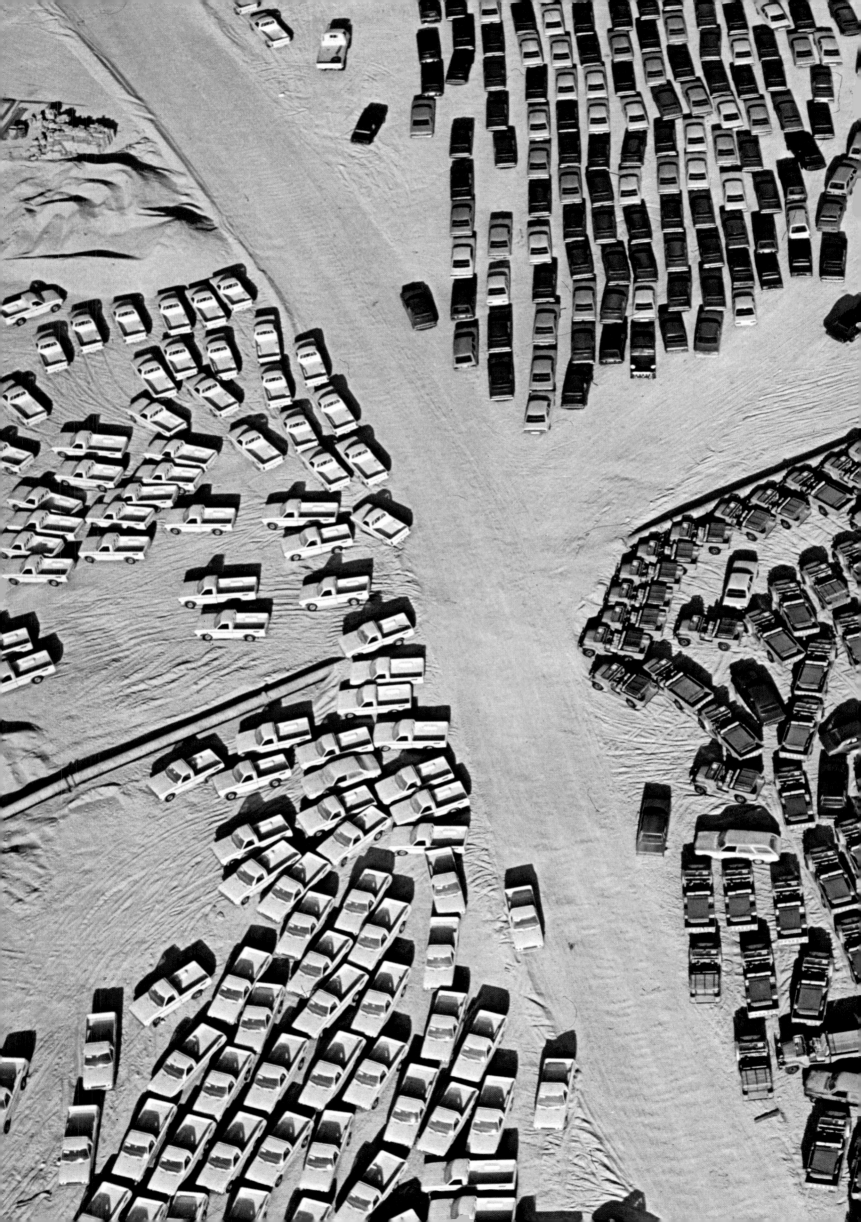

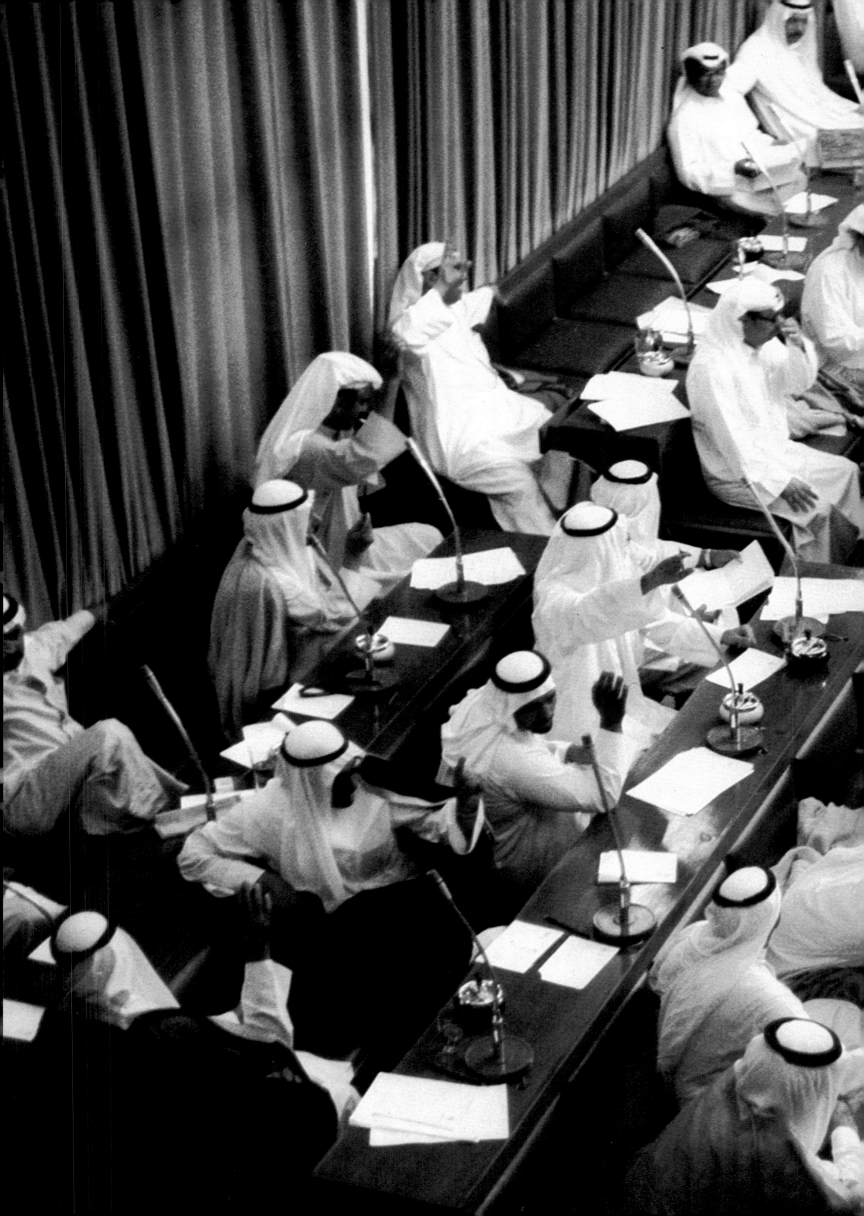

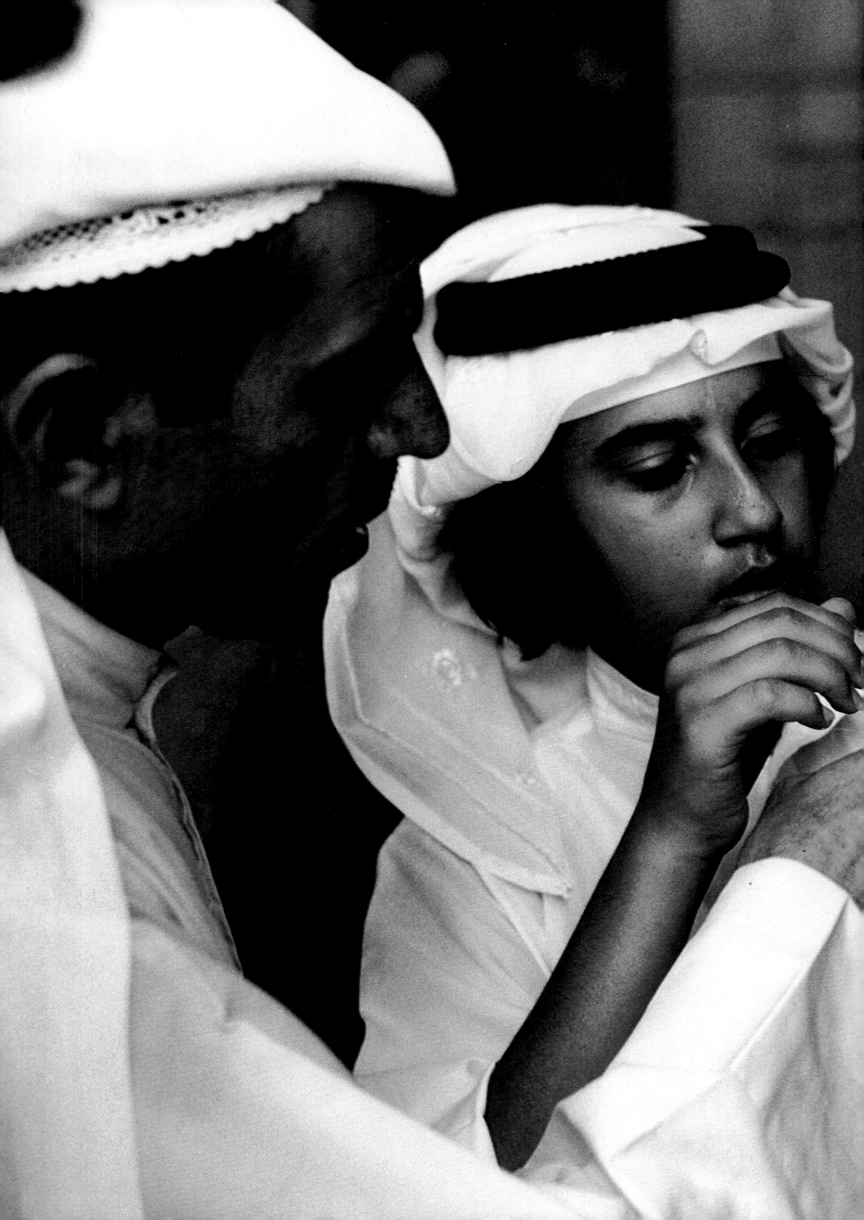

Photographs

209

Saudi Arabia

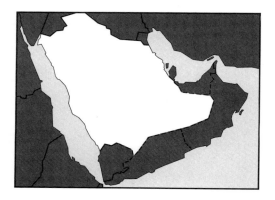

The Kingdom of Saudi Arabia occupies 873,000 sq. miles (2,260,000 sq. kilometers), or 80 percent of the Arabian peninsula.

To the north it is bordered by Jordan, Iraq and Kuwait; to the west by the Red Sea; and to the east by the United Arab Emirates, the Qatar peninsula and a section of Gulf coastline. Saudi Arabia has three neighbors to its south — the Sultanate of Oman, the People's Democratic Republic of Yemen and the Yemen Arab Republic — but in some areas precise frontiers between the countries are undefined.

Structurally, the whole of Arabia is a vast platform of ancient rocks tilted towards the east. The western part, the Red Sea coastline, is often mountainous while the Gulf coast is low-lying and flat. Forbidding arid desert covers most of Saudi Arabia and any development of the country seems a formidable task, not only because of the inhospitable landscape, but also because of the area involved.

The Arabian peninsula has great extremes of temperature. Summer is very hot and dry, often rising above 120°F (49°C) in the interior, while winter in the mountains can be very cold with severe frost. Humidity is low, except on the coasts, and rainfall averages a meager 5 inches (12.7 cms) a year.

Shammals, strong winds from the north-west, are often responsible for severe sand and dust storms in the late spring and early summer.

Arabia's greatest contribution to mankind, Islam, took root in the Saudi Arabian cities of Mecca and Medina. There, the Prophet Muhammad, born in Mecca in 571 A.D., gave rise to a religious movement that was to become, within two hundred years of the Prophet's birth, one of the world's great monotheistic religions.

By stressing the oneness of God and the duty of total submission to His will, Muhammad, the Messenger of God, gave rise to a religious/political force which by 750 A.D. had created an Arab empire which stretched from India to Spain, and which began five centuries of significant Moslem contribution to architecture, mathematics, medicine, astronomy and literature.

By the 18th century, while Islam continued to gain adherents, the Arab empire had crumbled and was in disarray. In Saudi Arabia, Muhammad ibn Abdul Wahhab, an orthodox reformer, gave rise to an Islamic revival that provided a moral and political basis for unifying the Arabian peninsula.

When Abdul Aziz ibn Saud, whose family had been early supporters of Abdul Wahhab's fundamentalist movement, captured Riyadh in 1902, it was the beginning of the culmination of a long struggle to unify Arabia, that ended with the capture of the 'Asir province in 1932 and the declaration of a new nation — the Kingdom of Saudi Arabia.

King Abdul Aziz ibn Saud died in 1953.

In 1964, Prince Faisal ibn Abdul Aziz became king. By reaffirming Saudi Arabia's role as the guardian of Islam's most important shrines— Mecca and Medina — and committing his nation to entering a new era of growth and development while maintaining fundamental moral and cultural values, King Faisal soon emerged as Islam's and the Arabian Peninsula's most eloquent spokesman and defender.

King Faisal was assassinated in 1975 and was succeeded by his brother Crown Prince Khalid.

According to the 1974 National Census, the population of Saudi Arabia is 7 million inhabitants. Other estimates place the figure much lower, but the rapid influx of expatriate labor, mostly from neighboring Yemen, and the nomadic nature of part of the indigenous population has made it difficult to establish a precise figure.

Riyadh, the capital, and Jeddah on the Red Sea, are the Kingdom's largest cities, with populations of over 500,000 each, followed by Mecca, site of the Ka'aba and the most holy city of Islam, and Medina, second holy city and the place where Prophet Muhammad is buried.

Most of the inhabitants are Arab, with some ethnic mixing apparent in coastal cities. Mecca and Medina also have large and diverse ethnic mixtures because of the large numbers of pilgrims who have come to Arabia to worship, study, work and perhaps die near the venerated monuments of their faith.

Prior to Saudi Arabia's emergence as a major oil-producer, the Hajj, the annual Pilgrimage to Mecca for the Moslem faithful, was the principal source of income for the Kingdom.

Oil was discovered in 1938, but full-scale production by Aramco, a consortium of four American oil-producers (Exxon, Mobil, Texaco and Standard of California) did not start until 1945.

By 1976, Saudi Arabia, the world's largest oil-exporter and third largest producer, was producing an average of 8.5 million barrels a day, with reserves estimated at 156,000 million barrels.

The country's economy is dominated by the oil industry which brings in 90 percent of the Kingdom's foreign exchange earnings and 85 percent of the government's revenues.

In 1973, Saudi Arabia acquired a 25 percent share of Aramco. After the 1973 Arab-Israeli war, and the subsequent oil embargo of selected foreign markets and the great «leap forward» in oil prices, the Saudi Arabian Government increased its interest in Aramco to 60 percent and by 1976 was negotiating for 100 percent take-over of the consortium.

The current five-year development plan (1975–1980) is designed for an expenditure of 144 billion dollars.

Development objectives are expressed in terms of maintaining the religious and moral standards of Islam, maintaining a high rate of economic growth, assuring the nation's defense and security, developing human resources and developing the infrastructure to support achievement of the expressed goals.

Saudi Arabia is an independent hereditary Islamic monarchy with the Koran and the Sharia, codified Islamic law, as the country's constitution.

Although there are no political parties, franchise or labor unions, there is an egalitarian attitude engendered by Islam that all men are equal in the eyes of Allah and any subject is permitted to approach the King directly at open court to seek redress to grievances.

Positions of power are distributed among the royal family and related families, and several members of the royal family hold important portfolios in the Council of Ministers, a consultative body which can initiate legislation, is responsible for the budget and has much authority in supervising regional and local governments.

Succession is limited to the sons of King Abdul Aziz ibn Saud. King Khalid ibn Abdul Aziz is the third descendent to rule and Prince Fahd ibn Abdul Aziz is Crown Prince and Prime Minister.

Kuwait

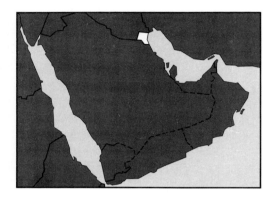

Kuwait is situated at the northeastern corner of the Arabian peninsula on the periphery of the Mesopotamian Basin and covers approximately 6,890 sq. miles (17,850 sq. kilometers) of flat and arid desert.

It is bordered on the north by the Shatt Al Arab, an historic area in Iraq where the Tigris and Euphrates meet the sea; to the west by the deserts of Iraq; and to the south by Saudi Arabia, with whom Kuwait also shares a very profitable oil-producing area called the Neutral Zone.

Kuwait City, the capital, is on the coast, built on slightly higher ground than the surrounding countryside and has a good, sheltered harbor away from the sandbanks and coral reefs which abound in the area.

The climate is one of extremes: in summer the weather is very hot with shade temperatures often exceeding 123°F (51°C) and in winter frosts have been known to push the temperature down as low as 27°F (−4°C). There is little rain − no more than 5 inches (12.7 cms) a year − and no rivers or streams, so drinking water has to be desalinated from the sea.

Kuwait did not become identifiable as a separate state until just over two hundred years ago when the Anaiza tribe, led by the Al Sabah family, was forced out of the interior of Arabia by a fierce drought and settled in the area of Kuwait.

By 1765, the settlement had 10,000 people, a fishing fleet of 800 boats, and an economy which revolved around pearl fishing and trading.

In the nineteenth century Britain's influence in Kuwait, as elsewhere in the Gulf, was significant. It was to Britain that the Ruler, Mubarak Al Sabah, turned for help when the State was threatened with invasion by Ottoman Turkey just before the turn of the century. In 1914, Kuwait's position was clarified as an independent state under British protection, although internal administration remained in the hands of the Al Sabah family.

Kuwait's present boundaries were officially drawn by 1922 and the Neutral Zone, an area then thought to contain oil, was established. It was fortunate for Kuwait that by chance the southern curve of the Neutral Zone boundary put Burghan, the world's largest oil field, in Kuwait.

Kuwait became completely independent in 1961, substituting the former treaty it had signed with Britain by one which promised British military aid if requested. This «defense shield» lasted ten years, ending in 1971 when Britain pulled her troops out of the Gulf.

Since 1965 the head of State has been Shaikh Sabah Al Salem Al Sabah.

Kuwait's population today is nearly one million, having tripled in the last fourteen years as foreign workers have poured into the country, attracted by the lure of high wages or displaced by political unrest in other areas.

While official estimates list 47 percent of the population as Kuwaiti citizens, other sources put the number lower. 75 percent of the workforce now comes from other countries: from the Arab world – Syria, Iraq, Egypt, Oman, Palestine and Yemen; from neighbors in the East – Iran, Pakistan and India; and as professionals and skilled technicians from various Western nations.

The incredible development of the oil industry during the last twenty years has transformed Kuwait from a small sea-faring nation with an economy dependent on boat building, fishing and entrepôt trade into one of the wealthiest nations in the world.

Kuwait sits atop a seemingly inexhaustible inflow of riches as revenues from oil pour into the country. 13 percent of the world's proven oil reserves are within its boundaries and according to present estimates, based on 1976 production rates of 2 million barrels a day, there will be enough oil to last for nearly a hundred years.

Oil concessions were first granted in Kuwait in 1934 and the large Burghan field was discovered in 1938, but drilling did not begin on a commercial scale until 1946. Production increased in 1951 when troubles in nearby Iran denied that country's petroleum to the rest of the world for three years. By 1956, Kuwait had the largest production in the Middle East.

In November 1975, Kuwait nationalized its oil industry, the first of the oil producing countries to negotiate a settlement that did not include a service agreement with the oil companies.

Kuwait's production policies in the future will depend on the amounts in which non-associated gas, or oil plus gas, can be found. The off-shore Dora Field, in the Neutral Zone, has quite large quantities of non-associated gas but before there can be any development of this area, an agreement must be reached with Saudi Arabia on the markings of off-shore boundaries.

The constitution of Kuwait defines the country as an hereditary emirate. The Ruler has executive power which he exercises through a Council of Ministers; legislative power is the responsibility of a fifty-man National Assembly.

Succession to the Ruler is restricted to descendents of the late Mubarak Al Sabah. The present Amir, Shaikh Sabah Al Salem Al Sabah, is the twelfth Al Sabah to rule Kuwait.

There is only one political party in Kuwait and only literate Kuwaiti adult males can vote.

The National Assembly was suspended by decree in 1976.

Bahrain

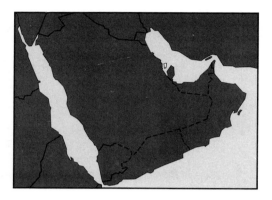

Bahrain is an archipelago of 33 low-lying islands wedged between the Saudi Arabian coast and the Qatar peninsula. The largest is pear-shaped Bahrain where most of the population is concentrated. Many of the other smaller islands have only tiny villages, or are deserted except for isolated fishermen's huts.

While most of the landscape is barren, with only a sprinkling of hardy desert plants, the northern part of Bahrain island presents a different picture: springs and artesian wells irrigate the area with water which slips along natural underground channels from Saudi Arabia.

For people used to hot, dry climates and desert harshness, spring water traditionally meant a chance to cultivate shady gardens, and those in the northern periphery of Bahrain island are notable. Today one can see large date groves in this area and many of the roads are lined with avenues of tall palms, heavy with golden-red fruits in the summer.

Climate is variable: summer, from June to September, is hot and humid with an August mean temperature of 88°F (31°C). The two months before and after this period can be quite pleasant, but winter is the best time of year. Temperatures in January average 61°F (17°C).

The attractions of Bahrain – abundant fresh spring water, sheltered anchorages, rich pearling banks and strategic location in the Gulf – were well known to the many peoples who came to Bahrain over the centuries.

Striking and unique burial mounds, dating from 3,000 B.C., today visible throughout the central part of Bahrain island, were mentioned by Roman historians and there is agreement among scholars that Bahrain is the legendary Dilmun, described as an enchanted mystery land in Babylonian and Sumerian records.

After many centuries of independence, Bahrain fell under Portuguese domination in 1521 and then under sporadic Persian occupation which lasted until 1783 when the Al Khalifa family, leaders of the Al 'Utub tribe from Arabia, succeeded in expelling the Persians.

From the mid-nineteenth century Bahrain had special treaty relationships with Britain, agreeing to abstain from acts of war, piracy and slavery in exchange for British support againlationships with a foreign government without British approval, agreements that remained in force until Bahrain became independent in 1971.

The population of Bahrain – about 300,000 – is composed mostly of Arabs belonging to the Sunni and Shi'a Islamic sects. There is also a large expatriate community of Indians, Pakistanis and Iranians who have come to the archipelago attracted by the availability of high wages and jobs. But, unlike other parts of the Gulf, Bahrainis remain a majority in their own country.

Manama, the archipelago's main town located on Bahrain island, has a population of 90,000, and another 40,000 live on Muharraq island which is connected to Manama by a two-mile causeway.

Oil was found in Bahrain in 1932 – the first discovery in the Gulf – and commercial exploitation by the Bahrain Petroleum Company (BAPCO) has continued virtually unabated ever since. 1976 production averaged 57,500 barrels a day and the known reserves, totalling 360 million barrels, are expected to last twenty more years. As no major new finds are expected Bahrain, unlike other Gulf States with economies which can remain dependent upon oil, has begun to diversify its economic base.

Fifty years of modern education in Bahrain have produced three generations of educated Bahrainis and the need to provide employment for its people as well as diversify its industry has motivated the government to create a progressive industrial state.

Bahrain has developed its own natural resources wherever possible. A large aluminum smelting works (ALBA), with an annual capacity of 120,000 tons, was built to use the Khuff field of non-associated natural gas. A vast new port, Mina Sulman, has been completed and a huge dry dock, an OAPEC project (Organization of Arab Petroleum Exporting Countries), is scheduled for completion in 1977.

On the financial side the Bahrain Monetary Agency is working to increase Bahrain's role as a center for international banking. A recent decision was made to issue limited licenses to «offshore banking units» which would be permitted to accept large deposits from central banks, governments, private investors and other banks in the area.

It is openly acknowledged that Bahrain's importance in the Gulf today is out of proportion to the amount of oil it possesses. Faced with a unique set of problems, Bahrain has skillfully managed to keep its place – its importance as a port and communications center has grown along with the power of the Middle East.

Bahrain is a democratic, constitutional state headed by the Amir, Shaikh Isa ibn Sulman Al Khalifa, a direct descendent of the Al Khalifas who drove the Persians from Bahrain in 1783.

The country achieved independence on August 1971 when all treaty arrangements with the British were abrogated by mutual consent.

In December 1972 elections were held for a constitutional assembly and a constitution adopted in 1973 provided for the election of a National Assembly composed of a fourteen member cabinet and 30 members elected by popular vote.

The Bahrain parliament was suspended, by decree, in 1974.

United Arab Emirates

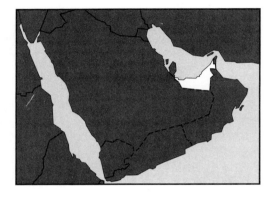

The United Arab Emirates, a federation of seven States stretching along the coastline of the Gulf and the Gulf of Oman, covers an area of approximately 32,300 sq. miles (83,660 sq. kilometers).

Except for the large oasis settlement of Al Ain in Abu Dhabi, all of the main towns are located along the northern coast. Sandy desert, dunes and salty marshlands make up most of the Emirates which are barren except for scattered oases. The coastal area has shallow seas, sandbanks and coral reefs, all tricky for shipping. The main port, Dubai, has long been the center of trading for the area because it has one of the few deep inlets or «creeks» where boats can safely anchor.

As in other parts of the Arabian Peninsula summer temperatures are extreme, often exceeding 120°F (49°C), but winters can be quite pleasant. Although rainfall is low—on an average of 0.10 inches (.25 cms) annually—humidity is high throughout most of the year.

The seven Emirates are:

Abu Dhabi: the largest in area and the richest in oil, it has taken the lead in industrial development.

Dubai: the Emirates' trading center; also the most densely populated, with an ever-changing skyline of new high-rise buildings.

Sharjah: the third largest, Sharjah is split into a number of noncontiguous areas and has dependencies on the fertile Gulf of Oman coast.

Ras al Khaimah: the most eastern of the Emirates, fertile, with considerable possibilities for agricultural development.

Ajman: only 100 sq. miles (259 sq. kilometers) in area, the smallest of the States and heavily dependent upon subsidy for development.

Umm al Qawain: quite small, this Emirate also depends upon fishing and subsidy for development.

Fujairah: set apart from the other States, Fujairah is located along the fertile Batinah coast on the Gulf of Oman.

The United Arab Emirates were known as the Trucial States until 1971.

The name Trucial States came about last century when Britain, then the strongest foreign power in the Gulf, signed «truces» with various Shaikhs along the coast after years of skirmishes over piracy. Harassment of British shipping would stop, while Britain would protect the area from outside attack.

For the traditional Shaikhs, the idea of a federation in the European sense of the word was alien to their way of thinking and there was no need of unity between the small states while they were jointly protected by Britain. But when oil was found, the concept of a State with defined territory became important.

When Britain decided to withdraw from the Gulf in 1971 many of the smaller Emirates were obviously not strong enough to be viable on their own. There was also fear that disunity amongst the shaikhdoms might encourage stronger powers to move into the area which was becoming attractive to outsiders because of its oil.

In 1968 the Rulers of Abu Dhabi and Dubai reached agreement to join together for matters of foreign affairs, defense, immigration, and social services.

They invited Rulers from the other Trucial States to enter into discussions and the Rulers from Qatar and Bahrain were also approached. Negotiations with these States proceeded for some time but eventually broke down. In 1971 six Emirates joined the union: Abu Dhabi, Dubai, Sharjah, Ajman, Umm Al Qawain, and Fujairah.

Ras al Khaimah, the seventh Emirate, joined a year later.

The population of the United Arab Emirates is estimated to be 700,000, an approximate figure because the first and only census of the area was taken in 1968.

Although most of the landscape is inhospitable, considerable numbers of people are now concentrated in the boom towns of Abu Dhabi, Dubai, Sharjah, and Ras al Khaimah. Abu Dhabi is the largest with 95,000 people, Dubai has 80,000, and Sharjah, 60,000.

Much of the native population is made up of nomadic and settled Arab tribes, but most people in the United Arab Emirates today are worker-immigrants. So many Pakistanis, Indians and Iranians have made the short trip across the Gulf in search of higher wages that they now outnumber the native population and their immigration has had to be restricted.

The economy of the United Arab Emirates is dominated by oil which, within a decade, has transformed a sparsely populated and undeveloped region into one of the world's richest countries.

The first crude oil was exported from Das Island, Abu Dhabi, in 1962. Since that time the United Arab Emirates has become one of the world's major oil producing countries, shipping high quality oil with a commercially attractive low sulphur content. Reserves for Abu Dhabi, the largest of the producers in the Emirates are quoted at 21,500 million barrels (1976). Abu Dhabi's 1976 production averaged 1.3 million barrels a day. Production in Dubai is limited to off-shore wells and the 1976 production averages 250,000 barrels a day. Sharjah, which only began drilling in 1972, had a 1976 production average of 60,000 barrels a day. Although new discoveries have been few, both on-shore and off-shore exploration continues throughout the Emirates.

The Governments have recently begun to press for ownership in all operating companies and negotiations are now proceeding for 100 percent nationalization.

Oil revenues have been massively invested back into the country. Financial and commercial sectors have been expanded, social services introduced and developed, and road and port facilities modernized.

Dubai, the main commercial center and entrepôt port for the region even before the discovery of oil, has greatly benefited from the oil boom. A tunnel and two bridges connecting the twin towns of Deira and Dubai have been completed and Port Rashid, a $ 50 million deep water harbor is now in use.

Work is also progressing on a huge dry dock project which will be the largest super-tanker complex in the Middle East.

Abu Dhabi has recently initiated major oil-related industrial projects including a gas liquefaction plant, a sulphur plant, aluminum smelter and petrochemical complex.

The Government is run by a Supreme Council made up of the Rulers of the seven Emirates. The Council chooses a President and Vice President from among its members and the President then appoints a Prime Minister and Cabinet.

The current President of the United Arab Emirates is the Ruler of Abu Dhabi, Shaikh Zaid ibn Sultan Al Nahayyan, and the Vice President is Shaikh Rashid ibn Said Al Maktoum, Ruler of Dubai.

At present the capital of the Emirates is in Abu Dhabi, but in the constitution there is mention of a permanent capital to be called Al Karameh which will be situated along the Abu Dhabi – Dubai border.

Qatar

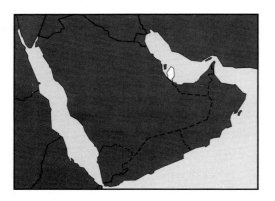

Qatar is a flat, arid peninsula which juts out midway along the eastern shores of Arabia. Over 100 miles (180 kilometers) long, it averages 40 miles (67 kilometers) in width and has a total land area of 4,000 sq. miles (10,400 sq. kilometers).

At the narrow neck of the peninsula, Qatar borders Saudi Arabia and its nearest seaward neighbor is Bahrain, about 100 miles (180 kilometers) to the north.

The landscape is predominantly sandy, stony, and barren. Natural vegetation is confined to the north, while in other areas only occasional date palms and sparse patches of camel thorn exist. In the south, there are sand dunes and extensive salt flats.

Limited supplies of underground water are available but are generally unsuitable for drinking or agriculture because of their high mineral content. Over half of Qatar's water supply is provided by seawater desalination.

Summer temperatures in Qatar average about 100°F (37.5°C), usually coupled with high humidity. Rainfall is slight and only in winter.

Archeologists have found evidence that people lived in Qatar during the Stone and Iron ages, but because of its extreme aridity the country was of little interest until the eighteenth century to any but the occasional nomadic herder, pearl diver, or fisherman.

In fact, an outline of the peninsula was not drawn into European maps until well into the nineteenth century, long after other parts of the Gulf had become regular ports of call for European trading vessels.

In 1916 Qatar, like its neighbors Bahrain, Kuwait and the Trucial States, signed a mutual benefit treaty with Britain ceding its defense and foreign policy rights in exchange for a British promise to provide assistance against foreign aggression. This treaty remained in effect until Qatar attained independence in 1971.

The indigenous Arab population of Qatar is thought to have come overland to the peninsula in the 18th century from the Al Hasa province in Saudi Arabia and from the region around Kuwait. There was also some migration by sea from neighboring Gulf States.

Those who came overland were mostly Bedu, and at least three well-known tribes can be identified in Qatar today – the Awamir, Manasir and the Bani Hajir.

Today over 180,000 people live in Qatar but fewer than twenty-five percent are native-born Qataris. The others, from various Arab countries and from Iran, Pakistan and India, have come to the peninsula to work as laborers in the oil fields and on construction projects.

Like their Saudi Arabian neighbors, Qataris are strict adherents to the Wahhabi sect of Islam.

Oil provides Qatar's main source of income. Unlike many other states in the Gulf, the Shaikhdom has no entrepôt trade and less than thirty years ago agriculture did not exist.

The Qatar peninsula is part of the Arabian shelf. Structurally, it is the same as the Saudi Arabian province of Al Hasa. Oil researchers noted these details and began to look into the petroleum possibilities of Qatar after oil had been discovered nearby in Bahrain.

Exploration began in 1937 and oil was discovered by Petroleum Development (Qatar) Ltd. in 1939, but it was not exploited until after the Second World War in 1949. 1976 daily production averaged 492,600 barrels. In 1974, the government negotiated a take-over agreement that gave it a 60 percent ownership of the on-shore and off-shore concessions and it is probable that the state will completely nationalize the industry in the near future.

Despite the oil revenues flowing into Qatar the Government is aware of the dangers of a one-business economy and has encouraged the growth of other industries to avoid total dependence on oil. But industrial production on the peninsula is still in its infancy.

Most significant of the new industries which have recently been developed are two cement plants, a shrimp-fishing fleet, an ammonia and urea fertilizer plant based on the conversion of waste gas, and a power desalination complex.

Agriculture is developing despite severe soil limitations and the harsh climate: while almost all foodstuffs have to be imported, the State has now managed to become self-supporting in vegetables.

Qatar is an hereditary Shaikhdom whose ruler can only come from the Al Thani family.

The present Amir, Shaikh Khalifa ibn Hamad Al Thani, seized power in 1972 in a bloodless coup by deposing his cousin, Shaikh Ahmad, a transfer of power approved by the members of the Al Thani family.

Qatar's executive and legislative procedures are controlled by a provisional constitution set up in 1970. A fourteen-man council of Ministers assists the Amir, and there is a thirty-member Advisory council.

Oman

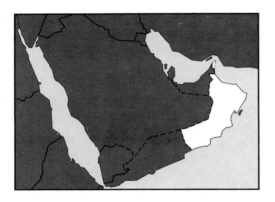

The Sultanate of Oman is located on the south-eastern shores of Arabia and covers 82,000 sq. miles (136,667 sq. kilometers). Flanked to the north-west by the United Arab Emirates, to the west by Saudi Arabia, and to the south-west by the People's Democratic Republic of Yemen, it is the second largest state in the Arabian Peninsula. A non-contiguous part of Oman, the Ras Musandam Peninsula, juts out into the Gulf at the Straits of Hormuz.

The border area where Oman meets Saudi Arabia in the Rub'Al Khali (the Empty Quarter) is not clearly demarcated. The country's coastline stretches for more than a thousand miles along the Gulf of Oman and the Arabian Sea.

Oman is a land of desert sands, high craggy mountains and windswept plateaus. The Hajar mountains extend over 600 miles (1,000 kilometers) through the central region of the country and rise to 10,000 feet (3050 meters). The most legendary part of these highlands is the massive plateau, Al Jebel Al Akhdar (the Green Mountain).

The climate of Oman is harsh. Summers are hot and dry with temperatures in the interior occasionally going above 130°F (54°C). The coast is usually cooler, but with a notorious high humidity. At Muscat, the capital, mean annual rainfall is 3.94 inches (10 cm) a year: in the hills of the interior it is much heavier — up to 15 inches (37.5 cms) annually. Oman's southern region, Dhofar, catches an annual monsoon from June to September.

Although most of the country is arid there is cultivation on the eastern coastal plain north of the capital. Land presently under cultivation in Oman is just under 100,000 acres, about 0.15 percent of the total land area.

Oman's early history is unclear, but there is archeological evidence of Stone Age civilizations existing in the area.

Oman was famous in Roman times because of frankincense trade from Dhofar to the courts of Europe and Persia, and the geographer Pliny described people from Dhofar as the world's richest.

Omani seamen, who reportedly developed the lateen sail, travelled far afield in search of trade and are known to have reached fabled Cathay – China. By the 10th century the coastal town of Sohar was perhaps the largest city in the Arab world.

In more recent times Oman was often subject to invasion. The Persians and the Portuguese occupied the coastal area on numerous occasions but they did not penetrate into the rugged interior – a region which remained virtually unchanged until the beginning of the 1970's, a surviving remnant of the Middle Ages. By 1650 the Omanis were strong enough to expell the Portuguese and by 1730 they had taken control of Portuguese settlements along the East African coast, including Mombassa and Zanzibar.

The country was racked by internal strife in the late 19th century and only the intervention of other powers such as the British helped keep a relative peace.

By the beginning of the 1970's the government of Sultan Said bin Taimur Al bu Said was regarded as one of the most feudal in the world. The Sultan refused to use his considerable revenues from oil, which had been discovered in Oman after World War II, for any purpose other than building up his arms supply and Oman was effectively isolated from developments which had taken place in the rest of the Arab world. Sultan Said bin Taimur Al bu Said was overthrown in July 1970 by his son, Qabus.

Oman's population of nearly one million is mostly concentrated along the coast within 180 miles (300 kilometers) of the capital, Muscat.

The people of Oman are mostly Arab, although in isolated places such as the Musandam Peninsula and the mountains of Dhofar some tribes speak non-Semetic languages which are thought to have survived from pre-Arab times.

Omani legend tells of two different Arab migrations into the country: the Yamani, who came from the south of Arabia, and the Nizar, who immigrated from the north.

Among the Bedu of the desert and the tribesmen of the interior there has been little inter-marriage between ethnic groups. But along the coastline, particularly around Muscat and on the Batinah plain, there are more mixed communities. The people of Oman were converted to Islam during the Prophet's lifetime. There are two main Islamic sects: the predominant Ibhadi, a strict austere sect not favoring an outward show of religion, and the Sunni, which is more moderate.

Oman's economy is dominated by oil which contributes 95 percent of the Gross National Product and most of the Government's revenue.

Until 1967 Oman had a subsistence economy based primarily on the production of a few agricultural products, fishing and herding. The marked changes to Oman's economy brought about by oil are recent; exports began less than 10 years ago. The main fields are at Fahud, Natish, Yibal and Kuwaish. Current production rate is 382,000 barrels a day and proven reserves in the mid-seventies stood at 6,000 million barrels. There is to date no heavy industry and the shortage of skilled labor puts a constraint on large industrial projects, but several ambitious plans are now underway or have been completed, including the construction of a natural gas fertilizer plant, a gas liquefaction plant, a water desalinization plant, a cement plant and a flour mill.

The largest single project so far has been the construction of a deep water port at Mutrah which can handle 1.5 million (long) tons of cargo per year.

40 percent of current land under cultivation in Oman is on the Batinah coast in the east, north of Muscat, where dates, bananas, and tobacco are grown. In the interior, the main crop is wheat, and in the southern province of Dhofar, with its strip of typical monsoon climate, coconuts.

Oman also has a long-established tradition of fishing, and its seacoast has waters rich in sardines, mackerel, tuna, marlin and sharks.

The Government is trying to assist these traditional industries and intensive research is being carried out to discover new crops suitable for Oman's climate. Fishing resources have been studied to find ways to improve fishing methods and to more profitably market the catch.

Oman is ruled by Sultan Qabus ibn Said, a member of the Al bu Said family, rulers of Oman since 1749 and one of the oldest dynasties in the Middle East.

When Sultan Qabus came to power in August 1970 by deposing his father in a palace coup, he inherited a country with a medieval mentality and medieval methods of administration. After the 1970 take-over, his government announced an ambitious economic program aimed at providing Oman with the basic social and economic infrastructure needed for a modern state. Improvements were immediately begun in education, health services, housing and communications. And for the first time a balanced budget was prepared for the country.

In 1974, sweeping government re-organization resulted in an 18 member cabinet, with Sultan Qabus retaining the portfolios of the premiership, defense and foreign affairs.

A crucial issue for the government has been the war in Dhofar, waged since 1965 against the marxist-backed guerillas of the Popular Front for the Liberation of the Occupied Arabian Gulf. More than half of the original budget was spent on defense. However, large quantities of new equipment and supplies, the political isolation of PFLOAG, plus help from some friendly countries, recently broke the rebels' hold over much of the Dhofar province.

Yemen

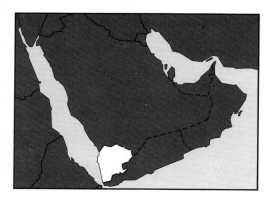

The Yemen Arab Republic, in the south-west corner of the Arabian peninsula, has an estimated area of 75,000 sq. miles (200,000 sq. kilometers). Figures are approximate because some of Yemen's borders with neighbors Saudi Arabia and the People's Democratic Republic of Yemen have not yet been clearly demarcated.

The Yemen has perhaps the most fertile land in the Arabian peninsula. There are two well-defined regions; the interior highlands, and a coastal strip along the Red Sea.
The climate of the highlands is probably the best in Arabia. Winters are cool and dry with occasional frost and snow, and summers are warm and rainy. In some parts of the interior the rainfall reaches as much as 35 inches (89 cms) a year, with most of the plateau receiving 15 – 20 inches (37 – 50 cms). On the coast, which is subject to sandstorms, it is much dryer with annual rainfall of under 5 inches (12 cms), but with high humidity during the summer months.

Two of the largest towns are set high in the mountains where the people benefit from the more temperate climate – the capital Sana'a, on the d'El Jehal plateau, is at 7,250 feet (2210 meters), and Taiz at 4,600 feet (1650 meters).

Yemen, the Arabia Felix of classical times, is the area where the fabled Kingdom of Sheba flourished (950–115 B.C.). From the time of Sheba until the sixth century A.D. the Himyarites ruled Yemen. In the seventh century the country embraced Islam, with both Sunni and Zaidi factions gaining control over parts of Yemen. Then, in the ninth century, the Imam Yahya Al Hadi ila'l Haqq founded the Rashid dynasty – a dynasty that lasted a thousand years.

A 1962 coup, led by Colonel Abdullah Sallal and supported by Egyptian troops, deposed Imam Muhammad Badr and plunged Yemen into an eight year civil war between royalists and republicans, a war that cost nearly 200,000 Yemeni lives and involved some of the world's major powers.

Army Colonel Ibrahim Al Hamdi, now President, led a seven-man military junta to power in 1972.

The Yemen Arab Republic is the most densely populated area of the Arabian Peninsula with 5.2 million inhabitants. It is estimated that an additional 1.5 million Yemenis live outside the country, most working as laborers in the economies of the Arabian Peninsula's oil-rich nations.

The country's most important export is people. Over one million Yemenis are currently working in Saudi Arabia alone, and the remittances they send home have an important bearing on the country's economy. Another 2 million people, or 80 percent of the labor force, is employed in agriculture, which accounts for 70 percent of the Gross Domestic Product.

Yemen's economy is heavily dependent on foreign aid, specially from its oil rich Arab neighbors.

Yemen used to be self-sufficient in food, but during the time of the civil war many farms were neglected. Today a wide range of foodstuffs has to be imported. The only significant increase in production in recent years has been in qat, a mild narcotic, which farmers find a profitable crop. Major export crops are cotton from the Tihana plains, and coffee. Both of these crops have declined in recent years.

Industry is still in initial stages of development and is mainly concentrated on light manufacturing and the processing of agricultural products.

Although a number of airlines now fly to Yemen, the country is still a remote corner of the world. Other forms of communication are limited; there are no railways, and by the early 1970's there were only 990 miles (1,650 kilometers) of roads, a third of which were asphalted.

However, some progress is being made. The main port of Hodeida, which was recently extended with the help of the USSR, can now handle 300,000 tons of cargo a year and the salt-shipping port of Salif is being rebuilt to be able to accomodate larger ships.

In June 1974, Colonel Ibrahim Al Hamdi, in a bloodless coup d'etat, came to power as the head of a seven-man military junta, ending twelve years of civil war and domestic unrest.

The government today operates under the powers of a provisional constitution that was issued six days after the 1974 coup.

Printing completed
November 1976
by DRAEGER,
Maître Imprimeur Paris.

D.L. 1976-4 - I. 7427 - E. 6732.